Be an effective DPO

Your guide to Data Protection Officer (DPO) role in General Data Protection Regulation (GDPR)

By

Punit Bhatia

Disclaimer

The thoughts and ideas listed in this book are aimed to help the reader with a perspective on DPO role in GDPR compliance monitoring. The thoughts or ideas are not legal opinions and shall have no legal liability whatsoever.

Further, the opinions, thoughts, and ideas mentioned in this book are the personal opinions of the author as an individual and do not have any correlation with any company or organization for which the author has worked or is working.

Disclosure

Copyright © 2018. All rights reserved. No part of this publication may be used, copied, reproduced, modified, distributed, displayed, stored in a retrieval system, or transmitted in any form by any means (electronic, mechanical, photocopying, recording or otherwise), without the prior written authorization of the author.

"Start now and you shall find your way."

-Punit Bhatia

TABLE OF CONTENTS

About this book i

Why this book? iii

Who Is the Ideal Reader of This Book? vii

How to make the best use of this book viii

Chapter 1: Introducing Privacy 1

Chapter 2: The Basics 9

Chapter 3: Principles and purposes 21

Chapter 4: Key Requirements 31

Chapter 5: DPO Basics 48

Chapter 6: Does your company need a DPO? .. 56

Chapter 7: Who does DPO report to? 71

Chapter 8: Skills and Qualities 80

Chapter 9: DPO vs DPO office 90

Chapter 10: Internal vs external DPO 94

Chapter 11: First three things to do 103

Chapter 12: What does a good DPO do? 114

Chapter 13: Being effective in DPO role 138

Chapter 14: Be effective in longer term 145

Annex 151

   1.   Job Description of Data Protection Officer 151

   Data Protection Maturity Assessment 154

   2.   DPO Stakeholder list 157

   3.   Sample Data Protection metrics 158

   4.   DPO Assignment Checklist 161

   5.   DPO Breach Notification Checklist ... 163

About the author 164

Acknowledgments 166

Make your own notes here 167

About this book

Data Protection Officer (DPO) is an important role in the context of EU General Data Protection Regulation (GDPR) and other data protection laws across the world. Appointment (or non-appointment) of DPO is also a key step in ensuring compliance with EU GDPR.

This book is designed to provide you with guidance on whether you need a DPO, who should he/she be, who should he/she report to, what skills are required and what are the tasks of such a person.

Further, if you are the DPO, this book answers your key questions like what you should do, how to become more effective and more importantly, how to remain effective in longer term. For those who have already assigned a DPO, this book will help you with a perspective on whether you made the right choice or you shall take additional steps. This book will provide answers to the following questions:

- Does your company need a DPO?
- What are the skills of a DPO?
- Should you hire an internal or external DPO?
- Who should the DPO report to?
- What are the key responsibilities of a DPO?
- How to become an effective DPO?

For all the above questions, if you need a pragmatic approach with actionable suggestions in simple and plain English, this book is for you.

Why this book?

With the General Data Protection Regulation (GDPR) taking effect as of May 25, 2018, there remain questions on whether a DPO is needed or what should a DPO do. Most executives understand that this new law will have a huge impact on their business, and believe that DPO is required, but they have questions. This is also important for those organizations that have decided to appoint a DPO but do not know what to expect of him or her. As they assure themselves, they look for a practitioner perspective.

Consulting firms continue to make money by bringing forth their perspectives like Target Operating Models and so on. The truth is that no one knows precisely.

And, that is where you need facts. The truth is, when you are challenged, you need simple and clear explanations of the key requirements about facts and challenges so that you can make your own opinions. This book has been designed and written with these considerations in mind and provides a perspective. And, this perspective is provided in plain English with actionable suggestions. Hence, this book is your solution.

In last three years, I have spoken to multiple data privacy experts and at multiple events on GDPR. And, I have always found the above as a recurring, common pattern. People are getting highly engaged with the GDPR articles and terminology, but consistently seem to miss out on the bigger picture and broader perspectives that are required in the context of DPO role.

At the same time, I have observed that people have been attentive to my thoughts and positively vocal in expressing benefit of what

I had to offer when speaking to them. This encouragement of colleagues and those whom I have met has encouraged me to share my perspective on what DPO role is, how it should be viewed, and what are the key elements of fulfilling this role successfully. Hence, through this book, my objective is to simplify the concepts and provide a clear perspective, critical success factors, and the actions. This is especially important now, as GDPR is effective. And, having this knowledge and broad perspective can be immensely helpful to you. For those who are still undecided on whether to assign a DPO or not, this will help you make that decision.

Finally, like my other books, the content in this book has also intentionally been kept to a minimum. I believe that once you understand the minimum, you can get maximum results by building on it yourself or through other sources.

With this, I welcome you to enjoy reading the easy way to understand Data Protection Officer Role.

Who Is the Ideal Reader of This Book?

The ideal reader of this book is any person who

- aspires to be a Data Protection Officer
- is already a Data Protection Officer and prefers to be more effective
- is an executive, project manager, program manager, senior manager, or business stakeholder who is keen to understand the scope, remit and responsibilities of a DPO.
- is doubting if his or her company would need a DPO or not.

How to make the best use of this book

Before we begin, I would like to suggest three points that will greatly increase the value you receive from this material.

First and foremost, I would recommend that you do not "see" this material as a book in the sense that it is something to be read once and put on a shelf afterward. To begin, read it completely once, then refer back to it if you take the role of DPO or as your DPO starts to operate.

Secondly, I would like to be explicit: this is not legal advice, but my personal perspective on GDPR. This does not have any correlation with an organization for which I work or have worked, but it is the total of what I observed and learned. Hence, expect this to provide you with the knowledge that you need to address the challenges you may have, and complement the knowledge you already have.

Thirdly, I would like to emphasize that this book does not replace the need for additional information for you but complements what you know while allowing for a structured approach to getting to know more.

To make it easier for the reader, each chapter has a "Pro Tips" section at the end. These guidelines will make your implementation quicker and more effective.

And, if you take care of above, I am extremely confident that you will gain a better understanding of DPO role, and what should be done.

Be an effective DPO

Chapter 1: Introducing Privacy

Objective: In this chapter, you would be introduced the concept of privacy, its history and a few laws associated with privacy.

What is privacy and why is it important?

It may not be obvious, but privacy is not a new concept as it seems. Ever since the evolution of mankind, humans have had a tendency to keep certain things to themselves or select few. For ages, men and women across cultures had a preference that certain aspects of their life be kept confidential or be shared with those whom they choose to. The extent of this personalization has always been dependent on societal context, personal preferences and cultural aspects.

The need to keep things on oneself or sharing with those who one intends to is usually called privacy. As per Webster's dictionary, privacy is the state of being apart from observation or having the freedom from unauthorized intrusion. So, without getting into words and meaning, privacy is about an individual being able to choose what to share about himself (or herself) and with who.

Now, the challenge in being able to retain privacy is that in the last 30 years, the world has become so much more connected. And, everything is readily available on the internet. This implies that there is a lot in the form of data. And, when this data relates to a person, we usually refer to it as personal data. Also, remaining in control is who this personal data is shared with and why is at the core concept of privacy in the modern world.

The history of privacy laws

Just like the concept of privacy, the laws on privacy have also been there for a while. Going through every law in each country is not the objective here, let us look at some of these.

- In 1950, the European Convention of Human Rights, or more formally the Convention for the protection of Human rights and Fundamental Freedoms, specified privacy as a fundamental right in its Article 8.
- In 1966, Article 17 of the International Covenant on Civil and Political Rights of the United Nations stated that "No one shall be subjected to arbitrary or unlawful interference with his privacy, family, home or correspondence, nor to unlawful attacks on his honor and reputation. Everyone has the right to the protection of the law against such interference or attacks."

Be an effective DPO

- In 1973, Sweden became the first country to pass the national law named Data Act. This also led to the foundation of Swedish Data Protection Authority. Probably, this was the first such national body for data protection at that time.
- In 1977, Germany became one of the first countries to introduce privacy law that provide citizen's protection of their personal data and put restrictions on collection of information for usage by companies that process personal data.
- In 1980, the Organization for Economic Cooperation and Development (OECD) published guidelines for protection of privacy and transfer of personal data across borders.

Be an effective DPO

- In 1995, the European Parliament and Council approved the Data Protection Directive that is commonly known as the Directive 95/46/EC. This provided individuals with rules for processing and transfer of data.
- In 2013, the United Nations General Assembly adopted resolution 68/167 on the right to privacy in the digital age. The resolution makes reference to the Universal Declaration of Human Rights and reaffirms the fundamental and protected human right of privacy.
- In 2013, the OECD also revised its privacy guidelines of 1980. This introduced a focus on the practical implementation of privacy protection through an approach grounded in risk management, and also the need to address the global dimension of privacy through improved

interoperability. In addition, this emphasized the need for privacy strategies, data breach notifications and the need for privacy management in organizations.
- And, of course, we have the EU General Data Protection Regulation which is the core of the discussions in this book. As we shall talk about it in the entire book, the next chapter is reserved for that.

Do all countries have data protection law?

The above list may give an impression that all countries have privacy laws and everything is fine. The reality is that most of the developed economies have privacy laws, but for the rest, there remain a lot of countries who are still not having privacy laws. For instance, even in a country as large as India, the highest court of the country (called as Supreme Court) is asking for a privacy law.

What are the challenges with these laws?

It is a fact that laws generally follow the technology and business evolution. Essentially, they generally play catch up. To the same effect, most of the data protection laws have been drafted in the past and need to be updated. As with the concept of privacy, the laws that govern privacy are also changing to reflect the modern world. Privacy of individuals cannot be governed by laws that are more than 20 years old. Reasons being 20 years ago we did not have: iPhone®, LinkedIn®, Facebook®, Twitter® or smartwatches. So, it is obvious that the laws are being modernized.

As laws get modernized, and implementation of privacy rules becomes more complex, the need to oversee the implementation of laws effectively becomes the most important thing. And, that is where the role of Data Protection Officer shall become very important. But before we start to talk about Data Protection Officer, let us hold back and familiarize ourselves with GDPR in next chapter. This is important because GDPR is one the latest data protection laws.

Pro Tips:

- Privacy is the need to keep things about oneself or sharing with those who one intends to.
- Privacy laws have been in existence since the 1950s.
- Privacy laws are continually modernized or refreshed to keep pace with the changing world.

Chapter 2: The Basics

Objective: In this chapter, you will learn about the GDPR history, its basics, and the key terms associated with General Data Protection Regulation.

Let us start by quickly aligning ourselves on a common understanding of what the General Data Protection Regulation (GDPR) is and the key terms associated with this law. This will allow us to swiftly move into the role of Data Protection Officer in coming chapters.

To understand the General Data Protection Regulation, it is important to note that GDPR is not a completely new law, but a harmonized, modernized and strengthened revision of the Data Protection Directive of 1995 (95/46/EC). Here, I use three important words. Let us emphasize on each of these.

Be an effective DPO

1. ***Harmonization*** created a single set of rules across all member states in the EU. Thereby making it easier for companies to comply.
2. ***Modernization*** made the directive relevant to today´s reality. As discussed in the previous chapter, in 1995, there was no iPhone®, no LinkedIn®, no Facebook®, no Twitter®, and the internet was in its infancy. Personal data, its privacy, and the risks associated with it were different. Comparing the two situations, the one of 1995 and now, are so different that the rules of 1995 can no longer be applied.
3. ***Strengthening*** because it provided what individuals need to be empowered with rights, and organizations need to be held accountable.

Be an effective DPO

Therefore, GDPR is a welcome change that strengthens the rights of individuals, puts accountability upon organizations processing personal data, and provides powers to Data Protection Authorities for enforcement.

For those wondering what do the words ***directive*** and ***regulation*** mean, in simple terms, a ***regulation*** is a law and does not necessarily need to be elaborated upon by individual member states; however, a *directive* is set of rules that must be elaborated upon and ratified as law by each member state. As stated, we do not need to get into legal aspects, but understanding the key terms is essential.

GDPR is a regulation. As such, it does not require ratification from member states (unless a member state chooses to be more explicit or stringent). It has become a legally binding law effective May 25, 2018.

Be an effective DPO

This means all businesses must enact fundamental changes to their data protection practices to ensure that their processes, policies, systems, and contracts conform to the new regulation. Let me assure you that if you that if you have been compliant with the directive of 1995, then the work is all about building upon what is already in place. Of course, there was a huge issue if you were not compliant with the directive of 1995. Sadly, many people I met at events state that they are not completely compliant with 1995 directive. Anyhow, I hope you've taken the right steps to be ready for GDPR. Let us stay focused on understanding GDPR before we start with the core of our objective which is becoming an effective Data Protection Officer.

GDPR is a set of rules governing how the personal data of individuals is processed and applies to customers, employees, and supplier personnel who are residing in the European Union. In GDPR language, these individuals are referred to as *data subjects*.

To form a deeper understanding of GDPR, we must first align on a few terms that will assist us in building a good foundation.

Be an effective DPO

Term	Description
Personal Data	Any information relating to an identified or identifiable natural person
Data Subject	An identified or identifiable natural person
Processing	Any manual or automatic operation performed on personal data
Controller	An individual or entity which determines the purposes for and means of processing personal data
Processor	An individual or entity that processes personal data on behalf of the controller
Supervisory Authority	A public authority in a member state responsible for monitoring compliance with GDPR

Table: Key GDPR Terms

As these are important terms, let us spend more time to understand these better.

Personal Data

To simplify the definition of personal data, GDPR uses the term *"personal data"* to refer to any information that can be used to directly or indirectly identify the *"data subject."* This includes but not limited to identification numbers, IP addresses, CCTV footage, etc. Further, personal data like race, religion, health, biometric information, political association, criminal history, etc., are further classified as *"special categories of data."*

Processing

"Processing" pertains to any operation performed on personal data. This constitutes any action like collecting, storing, using, sending, or deleting personal data. To be specific, collecting includes recording and

using includes retrieval, usage, modification, and combining or even linking data. So, if a call center has read-only access to your customers' data in Asia, then it is still considered *"processing"* of personal data.

Controller and Processor

As organizations process the personal data of data subjects, they are classified as *"controller"* or *"processor."* Controller refers to the organization or entity that determines the purposes and means of processing personal data (e.g., when processing employees' data, employers are considered controllers). Parties can be joint data controllers in certain circumstances. The processor is an organization or entity which processes personal data on behalf of the controller (e.g., IT providers hosting personal data for their clients are considered processors).

Supervisory Authority

"Supervisory Authority" is a public authority in a member state responsible for monitoring compliance with GDPR. This is typically a privacy commission in a member state. It may have a different name in each country. For example, in the UK, it is named the Information Commissioners Office, and in Belgium, it is known as the Privacy Commission. Sometimes, it is also referred to as the "Data Protection Authority". Thanks to GDPR, there will also be a European Data Protection Board which unites all the presidents of such local data protection authorities.

Who does GDRP apply to?

GDPR applies to all organizations across the world that process personal data of EU residents. Therefore, GDPR applies to all organization across industry sectors and

Be an effective DPO

around the globe if they process the personal data of data subjects who are EU citizens or residents.

What are the consequences of non-compliance?

Non-compliance with this law invites fines of up to € 20 million or 4 percent of global turnover, whichever is higher. Of course, these are maximum fines and a sanction would be applied gradually to an organization in violation of the law. For your needs, be aware that fines are significant and applied gradually. Legal counsel can help you with different details of the fines. My objective is to help you make a plan that reduces the probability of any fine(s) and demonstrate compliance upon official request. So, let us move away from fines and spend our energy on doing the right things.

What are the key dates in context of GDPR?

For those who love dates, the EU initiated a reform process in 2012, reached agreement on the new GDPR on December 15, 2015, and published it on May 4, 2016. Organizations were given two years to achieve compliance and must be ready by May 25, 2018. In short, the GDPR is active now.

Be an effective DPO

Pro Tips:

- GDPR is an EU regulation.
- GDPR is not new, but an extension of the EU Privacy Directive of 1995.
- GDPR is a set of rules about how the personal data of individuals is processed.
- GDPR applies to all companies across the world that process personal data of EU citizens and residents.
- Individuals can be customers, employees, or supplier personnel.
- The controller is an entity that determines the purpose of processing.
- The processor is the entity that processes personal data on behalf of the controller.

Chapter 3: Principles and purposes

Objective: In this chapter, you will learn about the principles and legitimate purposes for processing of personal data as per GDPR.

Now that you understand key terms and some basics about General Data Protection Regulation, it is time to build on our conversation and talk about core principles of GDPR.

Principles

The following principles are core to GDPR and must be understood for a Data Protection Officer to be effective:

- **Lawfulness, fairness, and transparency:** Personal data must be processed lawfully, fairly, and in a transparent manner in relation to the data subject.

- **Purpose limitation**: Personal data must be collected for a specific, explicit, and legitimate purpose. Processing must be limited to this legitimate purpose only.
- **Data minimization:** Personal data must be adequate, relevant, and limited to what is necessary in relation to the purpose for which it is processed.
- **Accuracy:** Personal data must be accurate and kept up to date.
- **Storage limitation**: Personal data should only be retained to the necessary extent. That is, personal data should be deleted once the purpose for which it was collected is fulfilled. Of course, certain applicable laws may require data to be retained longer. For example, most countries define a retention period for medical records in hospitals. So, in such

cases, those relevant laws need to be referred.

- **Integrity and confidentiality**: Personal data must be processed in a way that ensures appropriate security, including protection against unauthorized or unlawful processing. Also, data should remain accurate and consistent while protecting against unintended alterations.

Now, let us expand our understanding of GDPR further and dive more deeply into legitimate purposes under which personal data can be processed.

Legitimate processing purposes

As per GDPR, the legitimate purposes for processing of personal data can be:

- Performance of a contractual agreement
- Compliance with a legal obligation

- Fulfillment of a legitimate interest
- Protection of a vital interest
- Processing in public interest
- Consent of the data subject

Now, let us understand each of the above six types of legitimate purposes in depth.

Performance of Contractual Agreement – If the processing of personal data is required for execution of the contract that is signed between data subject and controller, then such processing is considered legitimate. For example, if a telecom company is providing SIM cards for mobile, processing of personal data to send invoices or bills would be considered as a legitimate purpose.

Compliance with a legal obligation - If the processing of personal data is required for fulfillment of legal obligations that a controller may have, then such processing is considered legitimate under GDPR. For example, the telecom company that provides you with a SIM card for mobile is now asked by telecom regulator to provide the list of all persons who have used mobile SIM cards, then the Telecom company must provide that personal data as this is for compliance with the law. So, this processing is considered legitimate purpose in category "compliance with a legal obligation."

Fulfillment of a legitimate interest – If the processing of personal data allows the controller to fulfill an interest of its own, then such processing would be called as fulfillment of a legitimate interest. For example, processing personal data to produce sales reports for management is a basic activity that a company must perform for running the company effectively.

Processing in public interest – If personal data is being processed for the fulfillment of public interest, then such processing is considered as legitimate under GDPR. This would usually apply to public-sector or government authorities. For example, this shall include the processing of personal data by government authorities to ensure the country and citizens are protected. An example of this can be government counting historical data for the purpose of prediction of population trend and may be in this category.

Processing for protection of vital interest – If the personal data is being processed while keeping the interest of data subject in mind, then such processing of personal data is also legitimate under GDPR. For example, if someone has a heart attack while being in premises of your office building, you may share his or her personal data for the purpose of calling an ambulance.

Consent of data subject – In case the processing of personal data does not fit into any of the earlier stated legitimate purposes, a consent must be requested from data subject. When requesting consent, the language used should be explicit and clear. Further, the fact that data subject has consented must be recorded. In case of processing based on consent, the data subject can withdraw consent at any time he/she desires. Once consent is withdrawn, the processing must be stopped. Finally, when consent is being requested, it cannot be linked to provisioning of any of the services agreed in contract (legitimate purpose).

An Example

As the above principles and legitimate purposes may feel a bit abstract and theoretical, let us consider an example to understand better. Let us consider a scenario wherein I subscribe to a mobile phone provider for SIM card with a company called ABC telecom services. In this case, the person getting the service is the data subject and ABC telecom services is the controller. As data subject, I would need to provide certain personal data like name, date of birth, ID card, email, address and so on. And, asking this data is a legitimate interest to perform the contract that is providing me with phone calls, mobile data and billing of same. Here, the legitimate business purpose is the performance of the contract.

Next, in order to provide me with regular connection for calls and data, the company needs to remain connected with my phone and keep tracking my location. This is a legitimate interest, but I as data subject should know that such processing is taking place. For this, the information in Privacy Statement on the website of the company should provide a clear perspective on what data ABC company has, what processing they perform and why. In case you think what this Privacy Statement is, I shall discuss the privacy statement and its relevance in coming chapters.

Further, the ABC telecom services should not collect any data that is not necessary for providing me relevant services. This shall mean data minimization. Similarly, the processing should also be limited to what is agreed in the contract and stated in the privacy statement. And, this becomes purpose limitation. Now, if the ABC telecom services prefers to make offers about their new products like internet at home, my consent should be requested prior to making such offers about new products.

Be an effective DPO

I hope this example makes things a bit clearer.

Pro Tips

- Map each of the personal data processing activities in your company to a legitimate purpose.
- GDPR principles are key to monitoring the compliance of GDPR on an ongoing basis.
- Accountability and transparency are the core of GDPR and can be recalled at various advice moments in tenure of DPO.

Chapter 4: Key Requirements

Objective: In this chapter, you will learn about the key requirements of GDPR. At the end this chapter, you should understand GDPR at a bread level. This will set the foundation for DPO actions and effectiveness to be discussed in later chapters.

GDPR requirements can sometimes be quite overwhelming. For this, I aggregate the GDPR requirements in 12 building blocks that can help you understand GDPR requirements in a structured manner. While you understand the requirements in this chapter, we shall come back to DPO actions per requirement in a later chapter.

Be an effective DPO

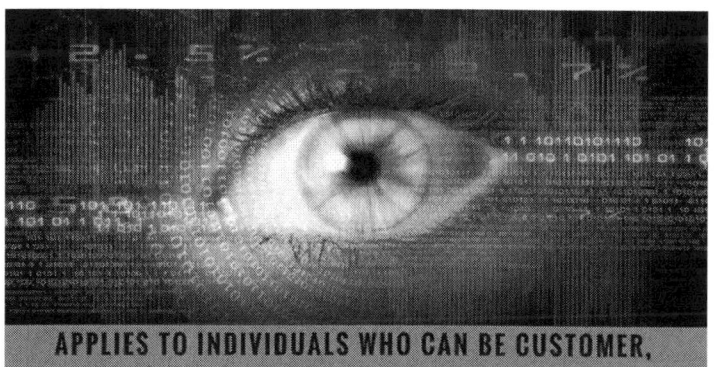

APPLIES TO INDIVIDUALS WHO CAN BE CUSTOMER, EMPLOYEE, OR PERSONNEL OF THIRD PARTIES.

1 Legitimate basis for data

2 Info you hold (retention)

3 Individuals' rights

4 Explicit and clear consent

5 Children's data

6 Privacy notices/statements

7 Data breaches

8 Privacy by design

9 Privacy impact assessment

10 Data protection officers

11 Third party management

12 Awareness

GDPR NON-COMPLIANCE CAN BE FINED UP TO 4% OF GLOBAL TURNOVER

Image: Key GDPR requirements

1. **Legitimate basis for data:** An organization must know and be able to prove that, for any processing it performs upon personal data, there is a legitimate purpose for doing so. For example, my internet provider has a reason to monitor my internet usage, because I signed an agreement to provide me internet and that the internet provider is entitled to monitor usage, send invoices, process invoices, etc. Similarly, an employer has the right to process employees' payroll, because each employee signed an employment contract, and processing of that payroll is a legitimate purpose as per employment contract. We have already discussed the legitimate processing purposes and businesses must ensure that processing of personal data is mapped to one of these. As DPO, one must ensure that your company

Be an effective DPO

keeps an inventory of personal data processing.

2. **Information you hold**: An organization should keep data only insofar as necessary. This means that if I paid back my mortgage fully, but now only keep a bank account, then the bank has no reason to keep my mortgage history, details of my assets, salary, etc. Of course, the bank must respect other laws that pertain to retention of mortgage data; however, the data should not be processed anymore. As DPO, you should ensure that personal data retention approach is defined and followed.

3. **Individuals rights**: To be assured that personal data is protected, data subjects have the right to ask what information one has about them and what one does with it, to ask for correction, to object to processing, to lodge complaint, to withdraw consent, or even to request

Be an effective DPO

deletion of their personal data (although the last is not an absolute right). This means I can ask my internet provider to tell me what data they have about me and request them to stop processing my data or even to delete it. As a DPO, your role is to ensure that processes for data subject access rights are defined and data subjects can exercise their rights.

4. **Consent**: When processing personal data, there should be explicit and clear consent from the individual. This means, if you wish to perform an activity like analytics for the purpose of making personalized offers, then the concerned individual should ideally be asked to provide his or her consent. As part of consent request, you must state what you will do with the information. For example, this means if the internet provider intends to monitor the type of movies I watch and websites I visit,

Be an effective DPO

then they should ask for my consent. As DPO, your role shall be to ensure that consent is asked in a simple and easy language.

5. **Children´s data:** For processing of children's data, GDPR requires the explicit consent of the child's parents (or guardian) for minors less than 16 years of age. In this case, member states can set a lower or higher age of consent, with a minimum of 13 years. This means, data processors should not send letters to my children just because they may know that I have children who may want to buy mobile telephones. As DPO, you will need to stay in touch with local law requirements about processing of personal data of children and advise your company accordingly.

6. **Privacy notices**: Organizations must transparently state their approach to personal data protection in a privacy notice

Be an effective DPO

that is easily accessible to data subjects. This privacy notice should have clear and easily understood language. For example, on their website, my telecom provider should provide me information on what data they have, what they do with it, and with whom they share it. As DPO, you may be contacted by data subjects as your contact details are mentioned in this type of privacy notice.

7. **Data breaches**: Organizations must maintain a data breach register and, based on the risk, the regulator and data subject should be informed within 72 hours of identifying the breach. For instance, if my telecom provider's systems are hacked, they should inform the supervisory authority and me if there is a risk to my data. A DPO has a key role to play in case of personal data breaches and we shall

come back to this in detail in a later chapter.

8. **Privacy by design:** Mechanisms to protect personal data should be incorporated in design of new systems and processes so that privacy and protection aspects are ensured by default. This means an organization should execute principles and guidelines to ensure that business and IT systems (and processes) are built to protect data subjects' privacy from the very beginning of the design phase. As DPO, you will be required to create awareness and provide advice on privacy by design.

9. **Privacy impact assessment**: When initiating new initiatives like a project, campaign, or product that would process personal data, the organization must conduct a privacy impact assessment to review the impact and possible risks. As DPO, you can be asked to provide advice

on risks that may be identified as part of DPIA.

10. **Data Protection Officers**: The organization should, in certain circumstances, assign a Data Protection Officer whose name and contact are published on the organization's website and identified by the regulator so that he/she can be contacted by data subjects or regulators if or when required. As this is the core topic of this book, we shall come back to this extensively in coming chapters.

11. **Third parties**: The controller of personal data has the responsibility to ensure that personal data is protected and GDPR requirements are respected, even if processing is performed by a third party. GDPR goes a step further in this aspect in that processors also have same obligations and liability as controllers in case of a data

Be an effective DPO

breaches. As DPO, third parties and data transfers are also a core of your actions and we shall come back to this.

12 Awareness: To create awareness among your staff about key principles on data protection, conduct regular training to ensure that the personal data of data subjects is protected and breaches are identified as soon as possible. As DPO, you have the responsibility to make awareness and training plans and execute them.

All of above can be summarized as follows: GDPR is a set of rules governing the treatment of the personal data of data subjects while requiring organizations processing the data to be fully transparent in their use of that data. To ensure compliance, GDPR empowers the individuals (data subjects) with certain rights and holds organizations

Be an effective DPO

accountable for their actions. The regulator is also empowered to monitor compliance, resolve complaints, and issue sanctions or fines in case of non-compliance.

GDPR through an example: Loyalty card

Let us understand these requirements using the following example to raise some interesting questions on compliance with GDPR from the customer's perspective. I choose the first example in retail industry because it concerns all of us. We all go shopping, which puts our GDPR understanding and relevance under the spotlight. Imagine, you ask for a vendor's loyalty card, which requires that you fill a form. Typically, a customer loyalty form asks for your:

- Name
- Date of birth
- Address

- Mobile number
- Email
- Signature.

Is all this data truly required? To the annoyance of some, I like to state that date of birth is not a required field. Of course, it helps to identify me, which can be argued as necessary. But, the reality is that the provider wants to know my age to build a profile on me but the exact date is not necessary. Instead, they can ask my age bracket which provides the same reliable data without being overly intrusive. Anyhow, let us assume I provide this information.

A few weeks later, I start to receive brochures of monthly offers from this shop that I got a loyalty card from. Processing data for the loyalty card was a legal purpose, and sending marketing offers can be a legitimate interest.

Be an effective DPO

I take no action to unsubscribe because I like the discounts.

This gets more interesting. In six months, I discover that the offers sent to me and my neighbor are different. This means my shopping behavior is being tracked through the use of the loyalty card. The question is, did I give consent to the processing of my shopping behavior linked through the loyalty card? Should I not have been asked before this action was executed? It is debatable if this personalization is a legitimate purpose or not. Again, let us assume that I choose not to act because I like the personalization and can receive offers relevant to me.

Let's say another six months later, this company's systems were hacked. News broadcasts state that all customers with loyalty cards have had their credit card numbers also hacked. This means my credit

Be an effective DPO

card may have been hacked and I need to know whether I should block my card. I go to the store's website to find information but find nothing. I call the shop; they state that such information details are not shared at the store level, they are sorry, and cannot help me. The hackers now have my credit card details and all personal information linked to the card, greatly facilitating any attempt to fraudulent use of the card.

Without piling on misery, let us see how this scenario would change if GDPR was correctly implemented. A compliant organization would have had the following changes:

- The data requested should have been limited to what was needed to provide the service. The actual date of birth was irrelevant to offer the Loyalty Card service and increased the harm caused by breach of security.

- The company should have made it clear on what grounds they would be sending me marketing material.
- The company should have asked my consent to analyze my shopping behavior so that offers could be personalized.
- The company should have sent me an email message assuring that my data had not been breached. Or, in a worst case, I received an email message stating my personal data had been breached, that the data was encrypted and that the risk of fraud was low; but, still, they advised me to block my credit card to mitigate any risk.
- The company should have published the generic information on its website, and the store manager should have referred me to a helpline where I can raise questions.

Be an effective DPO

Some of you may wonder whether all of this is common sense. Yes, it is. It is so common and ethical that everybody knows. Perhaps, we expect organizations to do all of this. So, why make the fuss if GDPR comes into effect and demands organizations to be ethical, transparent, and accountable—as they should be. And what happens if they are not, it is required to enforce the same through strong penalties and extended rights towards data subjects.

Next, as we align with Data Protection Officer role, it is very important to realize that data protection and privacy in the context of GDPR involves multiple aspects and can become complicated if not structured appropriately. Hence, I recommend considering a structured approach that is similar to what has been described in this chapter.

Be an effective DPO

Pro Tips:

- GDPR has many articles that can be overwhelming to understand. These articles are very useful, but I recommend using the 12 building blocks described above (or a similar approach) for broad understanding.
- Similar to the loyalty card example, create scenarios within each of your departments on how GDPR can impact you and demonstrate how you may need to do things differently. This will make planning your implementation easier.

Be an effective DPO

Chapter 5: DPO Basics

Objective: In this chapter, you will understand the need for a Data Protection Officer (DPO), the key requirements relating DPO role and the tasks of DPO as per GDPR.

Now that you have insights into the key principles of GDPR, its requirements and the legitimate purposes for processing of personal data, you may already feel that ensuring regular and systematic compliance to GDPR requirements can be challenging. If so, you have been right. Monitoring compliance with GDPR can be a significant work. This is especially true for companies that process personal data on a large scale or process special categories of data. Amongst other industries, this is especially true for industries like pharma, financial, insurance because large scale processing of personal data is involved. In fact, the services provided by some industries are solely based on processing of personal data. And, this is where the role of Data Protection Officer comes in.

When shall a DPO be assigned?

As per GDPR, a Data Protection Officer is to be designated by a controller or a processor when:

- Processing is carried out by a public authority or body.
- Core activity of a company, controller or processor, involves processing of personal data.
- Large scale processing of special categories of personal data is involved in a company's activities.

Be an effective DPO

While the above is applicable to all controllers and processors who fulfill above obligations, the courts acting in judicial capacity are exempted. Further, GDPR has the following requirements about the DPO role:

- A group of companies may appoint a single DPO if the appointed DPO can be easily accessible to each group company. This also applies to public authorities.
- A DPO can be assigned on the basis of his professional qualities. The knowledge of data protection laws and policies is a key professional quality in this regard.
- A DPO may be an internal staff member of the company or hired external who is on a services contract.

Be an effective DPO

- Assignment of DPO is not mandatory for all companies but needs to be decided in function of the type and scale of personal data processing.
- In case of DPO being assigned, the controller or processor appointing the DPO shall publish the contact details of DPO and communicate the same of Supervisory Authority.

Company obligations towards DPO

Another important aspect to understand is that if a DPO is assigned by the controller or processor organization, there are some responsibilities of controller and processor towards DPO. These are:

- Proper and timely involvement of DPO in matters of data protection.
- Supporting the DPO in execution of tasks.

Be an effective DPO

- Providing necessary resources for executing the relevant tasks.
- Allowing access to personal data and processing operations.
- Letting the DPO maintain his or her knowledge and expertise.
- Ensuring that DPO reports to highest management level in the organization of controller or processor.
- Ensuring that other tasks and duties performed by DPO do not conflict with his or her primary responsibilities as DPO.
- Not providing any instructions to DPO relating his or her tasks.
- Not penalizing the DPO for performing his or her tasks.
- Not dismissing the DPO for performing his or her tasks.

Further, data subjects can also contact DPO for matters relating personal data processing and for exercising their rights. And, of course, the DPO role is bound by secrecy and confidentiality inline laws of member state(s).

DPO Tasks

As per GDPR, the DPO shall have following tasks:

- To inform and advise the controller or processor and the employees about their processing obligations inline GDPR and other data protection provisions of the member state(s).
- To monitor compliance with processing obligations inline GDPR and other data protection provisions of the member state(s).
- To monitor compliance with processing obligations inline the data

Be an effective DPO

protection related policy of controller or processor.
- To assign data protection responsibilities, creating awareness on data protection and training the staff involved in processing of personal data.
- To provide advice when requested with regards to Data Protection Impact assessments.
- To be accessible to data subjects for their queries about processing of their personal data or exercising of rights.
- To cooperate with supervisory authority
- To act as the point of contact for supervisory authority relating issues of processing of personal data.
- To seek proactive consultation of supervisory authority when:

Be an effective DPO

- DPIA will result in high risk if mitigation measures by the controller are not taken.
- Controller has not sufficiently identified or mitigated risks.

Having come this far, you may realize that DPO role is a really specialist role. And, that is why in the next chapter, we get into skills of an effective DPO.

Pro Tips

- If you are a DPO, you must read the entire official GDPR text.
- Articles 36-39 from GDPR text relate to DPO and must be followed sincerely as day to day tasks.
- DPO role is an advisory role. So, as DPO, one should only advise.

Be an effective DPO

Chapter 6: Does your company need a DPO?

Objective: In this chapter, you will understand whether your company needs a DPO

Is assignment of a DPO mandatory?

Almost everyone aware of GDPR has this question. It is also a common topic that is debated at events. So, let us get this straight.

As GDPR, assignment of Data Protection Officer is not mandatory for all companies. This is a choice that needs to be made in function of the extent of personal data that is processed in a company. So, let us take a few examples starting from simple situations to more complex so that we understand this.

- A barber or saloon processing personal data for appointments with clients or keeping information about employees would not need a DPO because processing of personal data is minimal in relation to services they offer and also the type of personal data being asked is limited to few aspects like name, phone number and so.

- A grocery store would have a similar conclusion as for barber unless the store starts to offer loyalty cards that collect personal details like name, age or date of birth, home address and so on. Now, this may include systems in background that analyze shopping behaviors and so on. Here, personal data processed is more and extent of processing is also more. However, it is not absolutely necessary to assign a DPO. Again, it will change if we were to talk about a Walmart or Carrefour as in those cases, the processing is much larger and frequent. Further, more credit card details, payment details and much more information is being processed in such cases. If any of this information is breached, the company would need someone to engage with supervisory authority. Also, internal staff may need guidance on data protection topics. And, such operations shall do better with a DPO.

- A localized gym or a chain of gyms may be processing personal data for access to the gym, tracking fitness records of members and so on. Here, special categories of data like health data may be known. In this case, DPO may not be needed on a full-time basis, but a large chain of gyms may choose to assign a data protection responsible inside the organization

Be an effective DPO

but not formally announce him or her as DPO.

- An automobile company that produces cars generally keeps records of who bought their car, where they live and so on. However, they did use to process that data on a regular basis except for record keeping. However, nowadays, companies install black box type tracking devices that record, monitor and send data regularly. And, all these data are associated with the person driving the car. Some even make a profile of the person. As this gets more personalized and personal data processing is more at the center of their new activities, it is advisable to appoint a DPO who can assist in setting boundaries on what to do, and more importantly what not to do.

Be an effective DPO

- A bank or insurance company processes personal and special categories of data. Further, personal data is used to make day to day decisions like granting a loan, providing an insurance cover or not, reimbursing a medial claim etc. as personal data is being processed at large scale and is at the core of most services being provided, assigning of a DPO would be advised.
- A call center or payroll processing company providing services to other large company usually processes personal data to identify clients, understand their profiles, and respond to them on the basis of their product portfolio. Again, there is a significant amount of personal data being processed and at each interaction with a customer. So, assignment of a DPO

would be advised even though the company is a processor of data on behalf of another company that is the controller of data.

- A hospital usually processes personal data and special categories of personal data to provide services to patients. And, given the scale of its operations, it would be advisable to appoint a DPO. However, even though a doctor does more or less same operations processing of personal data, he/she may not appoint a DPO because the scale of personal data being processed is different.

What are the criteria to consider for DPO assignment?

By now, having been through different examples, you should have a fair perspective on what it takes to decide if your company

Be an effective DPO

needs a DPO or not. To make your choice easier, let us enlist the criteria that are relevant for this decision:

- **Does your company process a significant amount of personal data?** Part of this question, you should consider the types of personal data that is processed. As a guideline, remember that processing name, and contact of an individual is something everyone does but processing payment details, credit card information or health data is not common. And, processing data like payment info, transactions history, health data, etc. would be considered significant.
- **Does your company process personal data at each step of your service provisioning?** Part of this

question, you should consider how often is the personal data processed in providing services to client. If you recall from our list of examples discussed earlier, a barber or grocer processes personal data only for checking who is to be provided service but the service itself does not correlate with personal data. On the contrary, for an insurer, bank or call center, the personal data processing is being done as part of service.

- **Are special categories of personal data involved?** Part of this question, you should consider the usage of special categories of personal data being used or not as part of service being delivered. Here, the example of hospital comes to mind as health data, which is a special category of data and is at the core of service provided.

Be an effective DPO

Whereas, a call center may not usually be processing special categories of data unless the call center is for an insurance company.

- **Does your company employees consistently create new products and services that include personal data?** Part of this question, you should consider if your company's new products and services have personal data at the core of decision making. For instance, a new insurance product would always need personal data for making choices about a product but starting to sell a new product in a grocery store would not involve the personal data processing except that you may analyze overall client portfolio and see if the product shall fit the market or not.

Be an effective DPO

- **Does your company employees need regular advice on data protection matters?** Part of this question, you should consider how often do employees in your company need advice on data protection matters. An example to consider, maybe a grocery store or even large retail chain employees are less likely to have questions on protection of personal data of its clients but a marketing and analytics company studying behaviors of clients purchasing, movements etc. are more likely to need guidance and advice on how personal data is to be protected.

- **Does your company's clients expect your company to be protecting the personal data of their clients?** While this question is mostly applicable for service providers like call centers, IT service providers etc., part of this question, you should consider what the expectations of your clients are. If your clients share personal data of their customers with you and they have obligations on personal data protection, it is likely they expect you to demonstrate personal data protection procedure and would like to be assured that your company understand personal data protection and has put practices and processes in this regards.

Now that you have a fair understanding of what it takes to decide on the appointment of a Data Protection Officer, I am confident that you can make this choice. Again, let us summarize that appointment of DPO is not mandatory but to be decided in function of the

Be an effective DPO

extent of personal data being processed and scale of operations.

Next, irrespective of what decision you make in the context of your company, it is essential that you discuss this decision and its rationale for top management in your company and evidence the decision you make. The part of evidencing your choice is an important step to demonstrate that you have considered a decision on factual and rational basis to make an informed choice.

What if your company operates in multiple countries?

If you thought that decision of assigning a DPO or not, is a big challenge, let us think about companies that operate in multiple countries. GDPR does not put any restriction on assigning a DPO per country or one overall corporate-wide. And, in my opinion, this cannot be a binary decision that should be

Be an effective DPO

applied to all the countries you operate in. In my view, you need to keep in mind that DPO needs to be well versed with local laws in data protection, interact with supervisory authority, data subjects and your employees. So, before you decide, you should answer the following questions per country of operations:

- Is the operation in this country large enough by itself?
- Are the local laws in this country different from other countries?
- Would the staff in this country frequently need option and advice of DPO?
- Are there any local constraints like data subjects preferring to interact in local language only?
- Would a full-time DPO be necessary?

Be an effective DPO

If the answer to all of above questions is 'yes,' it is better to consider appointing a dedicated DPO is such country. If the answer to most of these questions is 'yes,' you may consider combining the DPO role for this country with another country or consider having a corporate DPO who shall advice all other DPOs in each country and also fulfill DPO tasks for smaller countries wherein DPO is not needed on a full-time basis.

For companies that operates in many countries and there is a need for more than a few DPOs, there is a good case for having a corporate DPO who shall set the overall direction and a consistent approach across the regional and local offices.

Pro Tips

- Appointment of DPO is not mandatory, but the decision is based on extent and scale of personal data processing.

Be an effective DPO

- Make sure to formally discuss and decide on the appointment of DPO (or not) in your company.
- Evidence the rationale for deciding to appoint a DPO or not.
- Appoint a corporate DPO if your company operates in multiple countries.
- If your company assigns a DPO, the name and contact details of DPO must be notified to Supervisory Authority.

Be an effective DPO

Chapter 7: Who does DPO report to?

Objective: In this chapter, we shall discuss the reporting line for DPO in your company. Also, you'll learn about a creative option to fill in a challenging role like DPO.

What are the options for DPO to report?

One of the most important aspects of assigning a DPO is who the DPO report to. While the GDPR states that DPO should report to the highest level of management in the company, there remains some discussion on whether reporting to Chief Operating Officer is the right option. Let us look at the possibilities and their pros and cons before getting into best options.

Reporting to Chief Operating Officer

Be an effective DPO

Reporting to Chief Operating Officer (CEO) of a company seems a logical option because CEO is the highest level of management and GDPR also asks for DPO to report to the highest level of the company. However, the likely challenge with this option is that CEO may not have enough time. Furthermore, CEOs may tend to focus on business than data protection. All the same, the advantage of reporting to CEO is that DPO has the necessary power or clout to cut the crap and inform of risks and bring advice directly to where it matters.

Reporting to Chief Operating Officer

The option of reporting to Chief Operating Officer (COO) is also inline law as COO is in executive management of the company and hence the highest level of management. Another advantage of reporting to COO is that COO is involved in operations of company, this is where the advice on data protection is most relevant. Again, one of the constraints of reporting to COO may be the level of interest and time available towards DPO.

Reporting to Chief Data Officer

Chief Data Officer is a recent addition in the management of most companies. Given that GDPR is about personal data, it can be a smart option for DPO to report to CDO. However, not all companies have a CDO. And, even when he/she is there, the amount of power and influence is not always there.

Reporting to Chief Information Security Officer

The option of reporting to Chief Information Security Officer (CISO) is a logical one since CISO is conversant with security, risks and breaches. In the event of a personal data breach, this can be invaluable. However, one challenge with reporting to CISO is that CISOs are not always in management board and does not meet the GDPR criteria of reporting to the highest level of management.

Reporting to Chief Risk Officer

As non-compliance with GDPR can create a significant risk to a company, a DPO reporting line to Chief Risk Officer can be an idea. The advantage of such arrangement is that CRO generally being in executive management, such reporting is aligned with GDPR requirement of reporting to the highest level of management. And, a CRO is usually well positioned to advice on risk, compliance and other matters which may crop up in GDPR. In my opinion, this is one of the better options and does not have any disadvantage.

Reporting to Head of Legal

GDPR is a law. So, DPO reporting to Head of Legal is a logical option for some of us. The advantage of this option is that legal perspective is put foremost. However, GDPR is more about processing and data.

So, who does DPO report to?

While we continue to discuss everyone in top management, we have discussed the most relevant roles in the context of data protection. As GDPR is about personal data and its processing, the decision should factor who is closest to understanding this and where this action takes place. Another aspect is that any decision or choice shall involve the understanding of legal, compliance and risk aspects. So, in my opinion, for large companies, it is best that DPO reports to a COO or CRO while for small or mid-sized companies, it is also a good option that DPO reports directly to CEO.

How about splitting the DPO role?

As there are two dimensions: one of processing and personal data while another of risk and compliance, there can be a creative option in large multi-nationals that generally want to implement segregation of responsibilities. In large multinationals wherein multiple layers of defense are common and it is preferred to segregate the responsibilities, it is best to split the DPO role into two. By this, I mean having an Internal DPO who looks after the business aspect i.e., processing and personal data aspects including transparency and advice to business. And, a Regulatory DPO who takes care of legal and companies dimensions by being the interface of the company towards regulator and external world including data subjects.

This approach has a distinct advantage that such approach splits the responsibility of a difficult role wherein finding one person who understands legal, compliance, risk, business operations, data protection and has a good communication can be a challenge. In this case, the internal DPO can be reporting to COO or CDO while the regulatory DPO can be reporting to CRO, Head of Legal or Head of Compliance. However, this approach is only suitable for very large organizations.

Pro Tips

- If you are a small or mid-sized company and you decide to have a DPO, a DPO reporting to CEO is the best option.
- If you are a large company, DPO reporting to COO or CRO is the option to be considered.

- If you are a very large company with a preference for segregation of responsibilities, it is worthwhile to consider splitting a DPO role into an internal DPO for business and regulatory DPO who takes care of the external world.

Be an effective DPO

Chapter 8: Skills and Qualities

Objective: In this chapter, you will understand the key skills required for a DPO role and the key qualities that a DPO must possess.

In last chapters, we have discussed key requirements and tasks relating DPO. We have also discussed the possible reporting lines for DPO. In this chapter, let us start with key skills and qualities that are required for being an effective DPO.

DPO Skills

In my opinion, DPO role is a crucial role for an organization and has huge responsibilities. For this reason, to be effective in this role, a DPO should be:

- Tacit communicator
- Intrapreneur by nature

Be an effective DPO

- Collaborator at heart
- Technology savvy
- Data protection expert
- Affinity to understand the law

As the above skills are loaded words, let us understand each of this one by one while relating to kind of work that is involved in the context of a DPO role.

Tacit communicator – DPO role involves communication with different type of stakeholders. These include:

- **Board members** – as GDPR comes with significant fines and DPO needs to report to the highest level of management, board members will be one of the key stakeholder group for him or her. The DPO must be apt passing the right messages and be able to provide right advice to them.

Be an effective DPO

- **Members of supervisory authority** – as DPO is the organizations' point of contact towards Supervisory Authority, he or she needs to be very skilled in sharing the right information in minimum of words and know when to ask for advice in a succinct way.
- **Employees** – as DPO needs to train employees and be available to guide them for their data protection queries, he or she needs to guide and be friendly at same time. Again, this requires a lot of communications skill.
- **Data Subjects** – as DPO can be contacted by data subjects for queries about data protection and to exercise their rights, it is important to have soft skills that allow interactions with data subjects who may be customers, employees or suppliers.

Be an effective DPO

- **Technical Specialists** – as data breaches and protection matters can be technical, DPO would need to have communication skills to engage with technical specialists.

If someone needs to be able to communicate with a set of stakeholders as diverse as above, it is evident that such person would be required to have very strong communication skills with capability to understand what is being said, and even what is not being said. Furthermore, he or she must be eloquent with words when speaking because his or her words would matter a great deal when advising board members or interacting with supervisory authorities.

Further, the communication skills of a DPO need to be top level for listening, speaking and writing because the involved communications shall involve listening and

Be an effective DPO

speaking to all the stakeholders we talk about and writing to the supervisory authority.

Intrapreneur by nature - as per GDPR, a DPO should not be provided instructions for his or her tasks. In this situation, a DPO is required to be a self-starter and independent who understands the dynamics of an organization and can steer through in different situations. Basically, he or she needs to have an entrepreneurial mindset while being in a large company. Like entrepreneurs, a DPO should be able to manage himself or herself in a company while making objective conclusions. Also, the variety of stakeholders that we discussed earlier will have a different way of tackling and hence needs to be self-motivated, action-oriented and proactive.

Collaborator at heart – as a DPO needs to talk to a variety of stakeholders, he needs to build relationships, find his or her way and be

Be an effective DPO

able to connect with people from various backgrounds, skills and levels. To be able to successful and effective in this diverse set of stakeholders, it is important that a DPO is collaborative. This is also important because a DPO role is an advisory role and not a decision-making role. Hence, it is very important that DPO is collaborative and brings along different interest groups.

Technology savvy – as data protection matters and data breaches are likely to be technical in nature, it is very important for a DPO to be able to understand technology and have some technology background. The DPO does not have to be technical but needs to be apt at understanding what technology can do and where technology can assist in resolving situations. Ideally, DPO needs to be able to make sound judgments on technical matters i.e., be technology savvy.

Be an effective DPO

Data protection expert – as the DPO role is about data protection, it is logical that a DPO needs to be an expert in data protection matters. A DPO does not need to be a lawyer but should be able to understand and interpret law while being apt at understanding the legal consequences. A DPO would need to understand GDPR in entirety and also the other data protection laws in member states in which his or her organizations operate.

Affinity for understanding the law – as DPO, you should have the affinity to read, understand and interpret law. By law, it is not necessary to be a lawyer by profession, but you must be able to understand GDPR as law, the local data protection law and any other relevant laws that may be necessary.

DPO qualities

Having discussed the key skills that are required for a DPO to be effective, it is now

Be an effective DPO

time to look at qualities that a DPO should have as a person. In my opinion, a DPO must have following qualities:

- **Objectivity** i.e., the ability to remain objective when confronted with different parties that have different interests. This shall be extremely necessary in situations like evaluation of risks from DPIA or assessing the need to notify data breach or not because you need to evaluate the interest of data subjects and your company. And the only way to do this right is to remain objective.
- **Confidentiality** i.e., the ability to keep and protect secret and sensitive information within the company. As DPO, one shall have access to information that is strategic and sensitive in nature. One shall also be

aware of new projects, products etc. And, in all such cases, being confidential about information is the right quality to have.

- **Ethical** i.e., being able to determine the right thing to do. At times, the law may not be very clear and may provide scope for interpretation. In such situation, being ethical would be a very resourceful quality for a DPO to have.

Now that you have gone through key skills and qualities that a DPO must possess, you shall know what to add to your repertoire if you are DPO. And, if you are reading to search for a DPO, you shall know who to look for.

Be an effective DPO

Pro Tips

- DPO role involves a variety of skills. It is important that your DPO has these skills.
- DPO needs to interact with variety of stakeholders. Make sure your DPO has finesse and skill of being able to understand and interact with such variety of stakeholders.
- DPO needs to be ethical and independent while being able to balance the interest of different stakeholders in an objective manner.

Be an effective DPO

Chapter 9: DPO vs DPO office

Objective: In this chapter, you will learn whether having a DPO is enough or he/she needs a team.

Now that you have understood the skills required to fulfil a DPO role, the pertinent question is: would a DPO be able to perform all his or her tasks, or he/she will need a team? Let us deep dive into this in detail.

Is one person DPO viable?

From the earlier chapter on DPO skills, it is clear that a DPO has a variety of tasks with varying complexity. And, the DPO has to manage a multitude of stakeholders.

Given, the job market, and availability of candidates, it is not pragmatic to expect one person to have the skills to manage board members, supervisory authority, employees and even the customers.

Further, you may recall that it is the responsibility of the organization appointing DPO to ensure that DPO has required staff. This is also an indication that even if you appoint a DPO, there is a possibility that your DPO may ask for staff.

Who should have one person DPO?

Barring the small sized companies wherein DPO role may be limited to advising management and working with the supervisory authority in some situations, most large companies would need to have a team of privacy professionals to fulfill DPO role.

Who should have DPO team?

For most large companies, it would be a DPO and his team. Already, the term Privacy Office as the team of DPO is picking up in

Be an effective DPO

market. And, in my view, this is the right approach as it allows for different persons to bring in different skills and complement each other to fulfill the varied responsibilities of DPO. This way, a senior professional can be the DPO while managing this team.

This approach of privacy office can also be a solution for large companies that operate in multiple countries. For them, the privacy office at a corporate level can be the central team that supports other DPOs, provides DPO services to countries that are very small and also lays out a common approach to data privacy and protection.

Pro Tips

- DPO role includes managing a variety of task and stakeholders. Finding one person to have such skills is not always easy.
- Small companies should have one person as DPO while large companies should

Be an effective DPO

consider the concept of a DPO or Privacy Team.
- Privacy Office or DPO team can be the solution to resolving the challenge of finding a DPO who can do everything and ensure that DPO has sufficient staff.

Be an effective DPO

Chapter 10: Internal vs external DPO

Objective: In this chapter, you will understand the pros and cons of choosing an internal or external DPO.

Once your company has decided that a Data Protection Officer is necessary, one of the next choices to make is whether to have the DPO as a permanent employee or hire an external consultant. Both approaches have their own advantages and disadvantages. Further, as the GDPR does not specify any restriction, it is primarily the choice of a company. Let us review each of the approaches one at a time.

An internal DPO

Even in case of an internal DPO assignment, you have two possibilities. It is possible to assign an internal staff as DPO or even hire someone as permanent staff and appoint him or her as DPO. If you choose to appoint an existing staff member as DPO, the person would have the knowledge and understanding of your company, its operations and culture. This can be a huge plus as it makes things easier in terms of working with the person. However, it is likely that the internal person does not have data protection knowledge and he /she will need training and this will take time for him or her being operational and effective in the role.

All the same, you always have the option to hire from the external market on your payroll and let him be part of your permanent staff. In this case, it is likely that the person shall bring data protection knowledge and experience. At the same time, the knowledge about your company's culture, operations and relations is likely to be missed. However, bringing an

Be an effective DPO

external into staff, you are choosing to invest in a person, getting a quick start on DPO role and ensuring a long-term asset for your company.

Irrespective of whether you promote an existing employee to be your DPO or hire someone to be your employee as your DPO, you need to be aware that it may be possible that your internal DPO is not independent and is biased in the interest of your company while providing advice on data protection matters. For this, you must ensure that the person being assigned has a strong character and can be independent and neutral while providing advice.

An external DPO

Asking an external company to provide you a DPO is an option that is frequently considered by small and mid-sized companies. This is especially helpful as they may not need a

Be an effective DPO

DPO on a full-time basis. This is also referred to as 'DPO as a service.'

DPO as a service option allows you to leverage on data protection knowledge and know-how of the person. Also, consultants are used to quickly understand the company culture, its operations and build relations with key stakeholders. Another advantage of an external DPO is that advice is very likely to be independent and neutral as there is no conflict of interest. The only disadvantage of this option is that your company shall remain dependent on an external company or person for a long time.

Be an effective DPO

	Assign Internal staff as DPO	**Hire someone to be part of your staff as DPO**	**External consultant as DPO**
Pros	Company culture, operations and relations	Data Protection knowledge. And, longer term benefit for having an internal.	Data Protection knowledge. And, flexibility to have the DPO on a part-time basis. Advice is more likely to be independent.
Cons	Data Protection knowledge may not be very high.	Company culture, operations and relations. Advice is	Company culture, operations and relations

Be an effective DPO

| | Advice is likely to be less neutral. | likely to be less neutral. | |

Table: Pros and Cons of different approaches when assigning a DPO

Be an effective DPO

How to choose internal or external DPO?

As both choices have pros and cons, it is a situation based decision that should be made in context what you are looking for immediately. If you believe that it is important to have knowledge and understanding of your company and its culture, you must assign an internal staff as DPO. If you believe you need independent advice and also DPO role won't be full time, the external DPO option is more viable. However, if you believe both data protection knowledge and knowledge internal dynamics in terms of company culture and operations is necessary, you should assign an internal person as DPO but assist and support him with an external consultant for few months. And, lastly, if the most important aspect is to bring data protection knowledge and you are willing to be patient with the person picking

Be an effective DPO

up the way your company operates, it is best to hire someone from external job market.

In short, key factors determining your choice would be:

- Company culture and operations knowledge
- Data Protection knowledge
- Part time or full time

Further, in my opinion, large companies and multi-nationals should always assign or hire an internal DPO while small or mid-sized companies may choose between internal or external on basis of need being full time or part time.

Pro Tips

- Both hiring an internal or external DPO have their own advantages.

Be an effective DPO

- Large companies and multi-nationals should always assign or hire an internal DPO.
- Small or mid-sized companies may choose between internal or external on the basis of need being full time or part time.

Chapter 11: First three things to do

Objective: In this chapter, you will understand the first three things that a DPO should undertake as part of starting his role.

What is DPO objective when starting?

DPO is a role whose necessity has become evident recently. All the same, GDPR is a law that has just come into effect as of May 25, 2018. So, as a DPO, it is very important to have the right start to your role. This can determine your effectiveness as a DPO in the longer term. So, as soon as you are assigned a Data Protection Officer in your company, you need to:

- Be clear on what are the key requirements of GDPR that are applicable to your company
- Get in control of what are the current risks and gaps

- Create awareness on data protection and mobilize key stakeholders

Now, the question is how do you do this. Let us take these three actions in a concrete way.

One: Define a Data Protection Policy

GDPR can be complex and not easy to interpret for everyone. As data protection expert in your company, it is your responsibility to make it easier to understand for everyone in the company. So, you should define a Data Protection Policy for your company. Basically, when in doubt, you want everyone in the company to refer to this document than anything else.

A Data Protection Policy would be an internal document that outlines what GDPR requirements are applicable to your company and what is expected regarding fulfillment of such requirements. Another reason for this

Be an effective DPO

document is that you do not want everyone in the company to start reading GDPR and have their own interpretation. This is especially true for companies that have employees spread across multiple locations.

A typical Data Protection Policy should specify the following:

- Purpose of policy to specify the key objective of the policy and let the reader know why this policy is created.
- Definitions of key terms so that terms like personal data, processing, data subject etc. have common definition.
- Principles of data processing to specify the guidelines that should be adhered to.
- Purposes of processing so that everyone is clear on what are the legal

grounds for processing of personal data in your company.

- Roles and Responsibilities that are defined to govern data protection and privacy in your company. Here, you should be explicit on how data protection issues should be raised and resolved.
- Requirements that must be fulfilled within the company when processing the personal data. Here, you should consider specifying the Dos and Don'ts.
- Controls that must be executed regularly to check if requirements are being complied with.

Once you have created a Data Protection Policy, get this validated by Management or Executive Board of your company. It is important that document has buy-in from highest levels of management.

And, if you intend to use this Data Protection Policy as the basis for the transfer of personal data within different companies or group of companies, you should also share this with the Supervisory Authority. If you do so, the Data Protection Policy will serve as Binding Corporate Rules (BCR) that allow your company to transfer data to companies operating within the same group.

Once agreed, put this policy on the intranet of your company and let everyone, especially the senior management know that this exists and must be complied with.

Caution: Before you define a Data Protection Policy, you should check if there is already a Data Protection Policy and if there is one, your task is to check if the existing policy is sufficient or needs an update.

Be an effective DPO

Two: Conduct an Audit

Once your Data Protection Policy is defined, you should conduct an audit of different departments in your company to check if the requirements stated in the Data Protection Policy are being complied with or not. On this, you may question the relevance of this audit as GDPR is effective and you expect the company to have run a data protection implementation program and be compliant with GDPR. And, it is exactly this assumption that I recommend you to test this audit. The idea of this exercise is to check if there are gaps between the current and expected state of processes and processing activities. And, if there are gaps, you want the same to be listed. Once listed, you shall evaluate the risk per gap and ask for closure of all gaps in due course of time. And, tracking closure of these

Be an effective DPO

gaps shall become one of your routine activities.

To conduct this audit, you have two choices i.e., conduct the audit yourself or ask an external company to conduct this audit for you. Both options have their own pros and cons. Let us examine the pros and cons of both these options.

Conducting an audit by yourself can be a very good opportunity for you to get a first-hand perspective on what's going on in your company. It is also an opportunity to establish rapport and trust with key stakeholders. And, more importantly, it will establish you as the authority on data protection matters. The only challenge with conducting the audit yourself is that you will need a lot of time and you may not have this as you have other tasks to perform as DPO.

Be an effective DPO

Conducting an audit through an external company allows you to save your time and provides an independent (or neutral) perspective on the state of things on the ground. In addition, you get to leverage on a proven methodology and tools that the external firm is likely to bring in. However, you should remember that this will require budget and you also miss the opportunity to connect with your key stakeholders across the company.

In my opinion, despite the obvious advantages of conducting an audit yourself, you should ask an external company to conduct the audit as it shall allow you to focus on your other tasks. However, I strongly encourage that you join all the interactions and meetings with key stakeholders and get a firm grip on what is going on in your company. This way, you leverage on the external company for what they bring in, but build a strong relationship with key stakeholders and also create an understanding of the situation on the ground.

Three: Define privacy governance

As part of your first priorities as DPO, you should create and establish clear governance. Having a clear governance shall enable you to make key decisions, create awareness on data protection and also mobilize key stakeholders.

The right way of creating is to identify key departments in your company. Usually, the key departments would be marketing, procurement, HR, IT, risk and compliance, key business lines etc. Once you identified your key departments, the Head of each of these departments is part of a board that would decide and steer the company on data

Be an effective DPO

protection matters. You may call this a Privacy or Protection Board.

Next, you will ask each member in privacy board to nominate a Single Point of Contact (SPOC) in their department. This SPOC would be your point of contact for data protection matters. As soon as you have created this network of a board and SPOCs, you have a layer to execute and another to monitor/advice. And, the first task of the members of your SPOC community shall be to create awareness about the Data Protection Policy in their departments.

Of course, before this community is effective, you must train these SPOCs about the key elements of Data Protection Policy, its purpose, benefits etc.

Now, the privacy or protection board and the community of SPOCs become key pillars of your data protection governance.

Be an effective DPO

Pro Tips

- Provide the employees in your company with clear guidance on what requirements relating GDPR must be fulfilled. For this, create a Data Protection Policy.
- Establish yourself as DPO by conducting an audit and getting a handle on what gaps exist.
- Establish a privacy governance by getting key departments to be part of your privacy board. This shall assist you in resolving data protection matters in the longer term.
- Create a community of privacy points of contact in key departments so that availability of Data Protection Policy and its monitoring is done through people in those departments.

Chapter 12: What does a good DPO do?

Objective: In this chapter, you will understand the different actions that a good DPO shall undertake as part of his role.

In Chapter 5 titled 'DPO basics,' we already covered the DPO tasks as listed in GDPR. Now, let us deep dive into those tasks by referring to different requirements of GDPR. For this, we shall use the 12 building block structure that was used in Chapter 4 titled 'Key Requirements.'

So, let us start by going through each building block.

- **Legitimate business purposes**: GDPR requires that personal data be processed only for legitimate business purposes. We already discussed legitimate business purposes in Chapter 3 titled 'Principles and Purposes.' As DPO, you should ask relevant business owners in your company to keep a register of data processing activities and ensure that this register is kept up to date. As DPO, you must advise the business on being in control of what personal data your organization has, which processes it uses, and why and how long that data is kept. For this, you may ask them to keep a data inventory. A good data inventory should answer the following questions for each data category:

- What is the business purpose of the process?
- Which legitimate business purpose as per GDPR does this business process match?
- What personal data you have in each business process?

Be an effective DPO

- What type of data is this? Normally, classifying personal or special categories of data is enough, but you may choose to define a deeper classification if you believe that it adds more value.
- Which data subject does this pertain to? Here, you classify whether data belongs to customers, employees, or supplier personnel.
- What is the purpose of this data? Consider making a standard list of processes that your organization carries out and map each data type to one of those.
- What is the role of your organization in the context of this data? Recall controller and processor roles we spoke about earlier. Here, you need to classify if your organization is playing the role of processor or controller.

Be an effective DPO

- Is this data shared outside the country in which it is captured? If so, you need to keep a record of the country to which it is transferred and may need to take other necessary actions.
- Who are the processors involved in this data?
- What is the flow of this data within the organization? Which applications process this data?

As DPO, you should not only insist on having this but conduct frequent checks and audits if such document is being maintained by each department. It may be a good idea to demand that this inventory is maintained in an automated way so that you have regular and need-based access to it.

Be an effective DPO

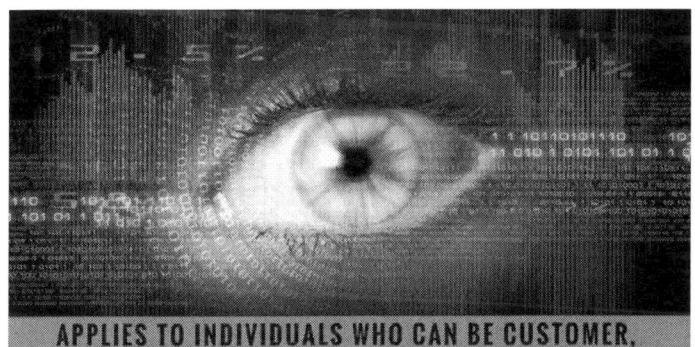

APPLIES TO INDIVIDUALS WHO CAN BE CUSTOMER, EMPLOYEE, OR PERSONNEL OF THIRD PARTIES.

1 Legitimate basis for data

2 Info you hold (retention)

3 Individuals' rights

4 Explicit and clear consent

5 Children's data

6 Privacy notices/statements

7 Data breaches

8 Privacy by design

9 Privacy impact assessment

10 Data protection officers

11 Third party management

12 Awareness

GDPR NON-COMPLIANCE CAN BE FINED UP TO 4% OF GLOBAL TURNOVER

Image: Key GDPR requirements

Be an effective DPO

- **Info you hold**: GDPR requires that personal data be retained only till it is necessary for the purpose for which it was originally obtained. In this regard, you as DPO should insist and advice to business stakeholders that they know:
- How long is each personal data stored? Specify whether the data is stored in paper or electronic format.
- How long should they legally keep this data? This is tricky and depends upon the advice of your legal counsel as you must choose which law applies. In case of multiple laws being applicable, it is advisable to apply the law with maximum possible durations.
- When does the data storage timeline start? This is also tricky because you need to agree with business and legal experts on when the storage period for this specific data begins.

Be an effective DPO

- What is done with data once it is no longer necessary for the purpose for which it was obtained?

As actions on personal data post retention period are not easy to implement, you should advise your company to make a data expiration approach. This implies consideration of following options on digital data:

- **Inactivated**: Data exists but is not in active processing.
- **Soft Delete**: Data is marked for deletion, but remains in the system.
- **Archived**: Data is moved to another system where it remains with access restricted to some key stakeholders.
- **Permanent Delete**: Data is destroyed and cannot be recovered.

Be an effective DPO

As you advice for data expiration approach to be prepared, you as DPO should insist on this being agreed upon at highest level of management. You can also consider using guidance from supervisory authorities. Some supervisory authorities have published guidelines on their websites. When you check or validate the data expiration approach, you should consider if the following questions are being answered:

- What action is to be executed once data is past the required storage or retention period?
- Who will approve such action and, on what basis? Normally, the agreed retention period can be a firm basis if agreed upon by relevant stakeholders.
- A decision on whether the expiration action is reversible or irreversible? Given the latest technologies, it is always

possible to reverse a certain action. Do you want such reversibility? If so, under what conditions?

- Who shall be notified when such action is taken? This is another challenge because you cannot say I acted on data once it was beyond its legitimate retention period. As you are accountable, you need to track all received data during the active lifecycle and notify them that similar actions must be taken on their end. And, it is this challenge that makes the permanent deletion almost impossible to execute.
- How will these actions be documented? This is very important. Imagine you remove data, but cannot track the action. If you are in a highly regulated industry such as finance or pharmaceuticals, then a regulator may ask you to prove what was done, when, and why. Therefore, having an audit trail would be handy.

Be an effective DPO

Doing all above would assist you in answering data subject queries when they choose to contact DPO directly.

- **Individuals' rights:** One of the key requirements of GDPR is that data subjects have the right to ask organization about processing of personal data. In this context, as DPO, you should check if the following rights are effectively implemented:
    - Right to information
    - Right to access
    - Right to rectification
    - Right to object
    - Right to object automated processing
    - Right to restriction
    - Right to portability of data
    - Right to be forgotten

Be an effective DPO

Further, as per GDPR, all rights requests should be registered. So, you should advise your company to keep a register or log of data subject access requests that are received. From time to time, as DPO, you should review this log and check if these requests are being answered within 30 calendar days of receipt of request. Based on local legislation, this time period may be different. Further, in the event of your organization requiring more time, this must be notified to data subject, or (his or her) legal representative in writing.

- **Consent:** One of the key requirements of GDPR is that when processing personal data for purposes other than for which it was collected, consent needs to be asked. In this context, your role is to advise business that Consent is always asked

Be an effective DPO

when necessary. As DPO, you should advise on when consent is needed. Normally, this should be an outcome of Data Protection Impact assessments. Also, ensure that there is a procedure to withdraw consent. Other things to keep checking are:

- Consent is not linked to provisioning of a service or product.
- Consent is explicit and pre-ticked boxes are not being used.
- The fact that consent was given or withdrawn can be verified. This implies a need to have some sort of record of the fact that consent was provided.

- **Children's data:** GDPR requires that children's data is not processed without the consent of the parent. While the minimum age is defined as 16, the member states can reduce this age to 13. Hence, as DPO, you not only need to ensure that children's data is processed inline GDPR but keep a tab on local law. And, if your DPO responsibility cuts across multiple countries, you should keep a view on local laws in this context.

- **Privacy Notices/Statements:** GDPR requires organizations to demonstrate transparency towards data subjects. This means an organization should create a privacy notice or statement. As DPO, you should check if all data subjects i.e., customers, employees and supplier personnel have access to information on what personal data the company has, what is processed for and who is it shared with. As DPO, when reviewing the privacy statement for advice, you should check if the following questions are being answered:

- What personal data does your company have about data subjects? Why is this data captured?
- What is done with personal data of data subjects? Basically, for what is the personal data used?
- Is this personal data shared outside of your company? If yes, with whom?
- What is the formal statement on retention, i.e., what is being done when data is no longer needed?
- How is privacy and protection of personal data ensured?
- How can a data subject exercise his or her rights?
- Whom do data subject contact to know more or lodge a complaint? Normally, this section should contain contact details of DPO. Now, to protect your personal identity, I always prefer that you use a

generic mail like privacy@abc.com or dpo@mycompany.com.

In addition, you should ask for this statement to written in a plain and simple language without any technical jargon.

- **Data Breaches:** A personal data breach is one of the key activities in which a DPO is at the center of communication. As it is the responsibility of a DPO to notify the supervisory authority and data subjects (if needed), it is key for a DPO to have templates for notifying the supervisory authority and data subjects ready. As a personal data breach needs to be notified within 72 hours of being known, it is important to be prepared. It is important to recall that if you are a DPO for an organization that plays the role of a processor, the breach notification should only be sent to DPO of controller.

Be an effective DPO

When notifying to a supervisory authority (or DPO of controller, if your company is playing the role of a processor), the DPO should include the following information:

- Number of personal records impacted
- Number of data subjects impacted
- Name and contact information of Data Protection Officer
- Description of likely impact of the data breach
- Proactive description of measures that were in place to prevent such breaches

Once a breach is contained, it is important for DPO to organize and record the lessons learned. If required, a DPO should also advise on the new measures that the company should take to prevent reoccurrence.

Be an effective DPO

Further, as DPO, you must make and keep a data breach register. This breach register should ideally include:

- The date and time on which the personal data breach was identified
- The source of information about the personal data breach. This can be the person who identified or processor who notified if you are a controller.
- Number of personal data records impacted
- Number of data subjects impacted
- The date and time at which the supervisory authority was notified
- The date and time at which data subjects were notified
- The reason for not notifying a personal data breach to supervisory authority, if the choice was not to notify

- The identified reason for personal data breach
- The lessons learned and new actions taken

As a DPO, this record keeping of data breaches and documentation is key to your being an effective DPO.

- **Privacy by design:** Privacy by design and default are two concepts that a DPO must inform the relevant employees of his or her company. In this area, the role of DPO is to create awareness about these topics and advice relevant stakeholders like enterprise and system architects to formulate guidelines and checks so that new processes, systems and products are inherently compliant to privacy by design. Another role of DPO in this context is to provide advice on these matters when asked for.

Be an effective DPO

- **Privacy Impact Assessments:** Privacy Impact Assessments should be conducted by your company to identify if the new process or product would result in a risk for freedom and rights of data subjects. In this context, a DPO role is to advise and assist in creation of a DPIA template and process if that does not exist already. A DPO should also conduct training on how to conduct DPIA.

Also, when a new processing activity or a change to existing processing activity results in a risk to rights and freedoms of data subjects, the DPO should provide advice to his or her company on necessary mitigation actions. As per GDPR, a DPO may also consult the supervisory authority for advice if the risk to rights and freedoms of data subjects is perceived to be high. As like other areas of involvement, DPIAs should be registered in log and advice of DPO recorded as evidence.

- **Data Protection Officer:** As a DPO, this is the requirement you fulfil and the only thing I can advise here is that you make sure you have necessary staff and budget. Further, like all other requirements, you shall keep an evidence of actions in this context.

- **Third Party management:** Data transfers within the company when offices are located in different countries and outside for processing with third parties are important areas in the remit of personal data protection. In these, advice and input of DPO plays an important part.

For data transfers within the company entities, you can rely on contractual clauses or Binding Corporate Rules (BCR). In intracompany context, BCRs can save a lot of time and effort in having to write contracts for data transfers in company context. So, for large multinationals, BCR is the recommended option.

As for external contracts with third parties, your role as DPO shall be determined based on DPIA outcome. Of course, you need to advise that DPIA is conducted if it has not been conducted. Further, for third party contracts, you shall undertake two actions:

    a. Ask the legal counsel in your company to draft data protection clauses for inclusion in contracts that involve personal data. As you review these for advice, check that adequate provisions to protect personal data, notification of breach and processing of personal data are listed in those. Normally, your legal counsel shall rely on EU Model contract clauses for this purpose.

b. Ask your procurement or risk teams to include data protection elements in the supplier audits that they conduct. And, if no audits are in place, it is time to ask for a procedure and approach to conduct the supplier audits on third parties that are processing personal data for your company.

- **Awareness:** A core part of your role as DPO is to ensure that employees in your organization understand the importance of data privacy and protection. Essentially, you need to ensure that data privacy and protection principles and processes are embedded in the day-to-day activities of your business. This

Be an effective DPO

challenging aspect calls for implementing a culture (change) of privacy and ethics. While this is also a legal requirement, you need to build a comprehensive approach to cover:

- Creation of awareness to ensure that all staff understand that privacy and protection of personal data are aware of the role they play in keeping the organization GDPR compliance

- Creating and providing basic information about data protection (and privacy) principles to clarify department-specific guidelines.

While you make plans to create awareness and provide training, it is important to put in place mechanisms to measure the privacy knowledge in your company. For this, ideas

Be an effective DPO

like conducting quizzes, asking attendees to answer questionnaires and providing certifications based on exams should be considered. Finally, the training and awareness should be repeated regularly. In my opinion, the training should be repeated every year.

Pro Tips

- To effectively oversee the data protection practices in your company, you need a set of tasks linked to each GDPR requirement. For this, you should structure the GDPR requirements into a page. Of course, I prefer the 12 block structure that is shared in this book.
- As DPO tasks spread over a number of areas, DPO should focus on advising what to do and review of proposed way of working.

Be an effective DPO

Chapter 13: Being effective in DPO role

Objective: In this chapter, you will understand the critical success factors in terms of the do's, the don'ts, and the common mistakes that one can make while being a Data Protection Officer.

Now that you have insight into the key aspects of GDPR, your role, skills and tasks. Let us discuss the critical success factors that will assist you in doing the right things and help in avoiding mistakes.

1. **Create a privacy dashboard**: it is said that you cannot manage what you don't measure. This is also true in privacy and your role as DPO. So, I recommend you create a dashboard of key metrics and review it on a weekly basis. Doing so will assist you in

Be an effective DPO

gaining perspective on what's going on and where there is a need for additional focus. In my opinion, you should measure the following on weekly and monthly basis:

    a. Number of personal data breaches

    b. Number of data breaches reported to DPA

    c. Number of Data Subject Access Requests (DSAR)*

    d. Number of complaints to Data Protection Authority

    e. % of new clients who provided consent

    f. Number of reactions of privacy statement

    g. Number of open high-risk items from last data protection audit

h. Number of open risk items from last data protection audit

*may measure this per DSAR

2. **Evidence the actions** – it has been stated many times in this book but this is a critical success factor. You must evidence all decisions that are made in the context of data protection and the advice you made. The idea is not to be protective of oneself but has validation that right inputs were provided, considered and rationale for decisions that were made. Such evidence can be immensely helpful when your company is audited by a Supervisory Authority.

3. **Be an independent advisor** – your role as DPO is to monitor compliance and provide independent advice. Do not make decisions, but provide inputs

and options so that decisions can be made. And, keep this advice independent of any commercial interests of the company and do not be under any pressure, whatsoever.

4. **Use GDPR as your framework** – while your company's data protection policy is prepared for employees, you should also look to GDPR as the framework that guides you for key topics. This is in addition to your internal policy and not in place of your policy. I recommend not to see GDPR as the ceiling under which your organization should fit, but a floor on which you shall build the data protection practices and culture of your company so that your customers can do more business with your company with increased trust that your company shall protect their data.

5. **Factor other laws** – compliance with GDPR shall require being aware of other laws. For example, when deciding on how long to retain personal data, the decision shall be on law other than GDPR. So, remain open to being aware of other laws and seek the advice of legal counsel in your company.

6. **Focus on the longer term** - Compliance with the law and avoidance of fines are certainly important, but only focusing on those sets yourself up for challenges in the longer term. So, I strongly recommend taking a longer-term perspective and considering to have a maturity model that allows you to embed a continuous improvement culture in data protection in your company. An indicative data

protection maturity model is provided in Annex for your reference.

In summary, being an effective DPO is not about working from a fixed list of one-off compliance actions but about strategic and continuous involvement in governance with a view on a longer-term impact on your business. The more you engage your employees and customers through a transparency approach, the more likely that your company wins more business by differentiation from the competition. Be aware that GDPR will impact all layers of your organization; i.e., it will impact the processes, policies, governance, and even your organizational structure. So, your role as DPO is to continually review if each of these aspects is doing the right things in terms of data protection.

Be an effective DPO

Pro Tips

- DPO role is not about one-off compliance actions but concerns a longer-term perspective on monitoring processes, policies and governance to be effective in data protection.
- Review your data protection approach, policy and procedures on a regular basis. Ideally, every one or two years.

Chapter 14: Be effective in longer term

Objective: In this chapter, you will learn about the key actions that you should take to remain an effective Data Protection Officer in the longer term.

As we come towards the end, it is important to discuss certain actions that will make sure that you remain effective as time passes by. In my opinion, there needs to be a balance between day to day and future focus. From my perspective, a DPO should take the following actions:

- **Training and certification** – A DPO should identify the best training and certifications and subscribe to them from time to time. This shall ensure that your skills remain up to date. Part of this, you should not only focus on

Be an effective DPO

training on data protection but also on soft skills like influencing others, communication skills, being independent etc.

- **"Join a DPO community or network"** – Like any other job, there are others in the world who have similar challenges and there is no better way than to go and discuss with others. This is a very effective way of sharing challenges and best practices. I advise you to join a DPO community or network in your city or region.
- **Subscribe newsletters** – To remain up to date with trends and new developments; you must subscribe to a few data protection newsletters. I won't provide publicity to ones I use but do not hesitate to connect with me and ask for this.

- **Attend events** – While joining communities and subscribing newsletters are good ideas, attending events cannot be ignored. Stay on a lookout for events and attend them. I recommend attending at least one event a quarter
- **Spend time on the internet yourself** – While you shall get info from other sources, doing your own research cannot be understated. You need to stay a step ahead. So, spend some time to research yourself once in a while. For example, we all know e-Privacy regulation is in the draft. And, reading about that can only be beneficial.

In short, the message is to go out to connect, engage and share so that you continuing looking forward to what is happening next. This is very necessary to remain effective.

Pro Tips

- Invest in yourself.
- Markets and trends evolve. Change is the only constant. I know you are busy and there are a lot of tasks to do. But you must set aside time in advance.
- Go out and meet colleagues in the same profession. You will be enriched with their experiences and find solutions to your challenges.

One last thing…

Privacy is a topic that is evolving very fast. In my view, in the next five years or so, we will witness a lot of new developments, like availability of privacy certifications for companies, new solutions, and tools to make it easier to comply with GDPR and e-Privacy regulations. If you are working on this topic, enjoy the development of these new skills, because privacy is most likely here to stay because data will continue to become more digital. The more digital data becomes, the more relevant the privacy aspect becomes.

With this, I like to thank you for buying this book and taking your valuable time to read it. I sincerely hope that you found this book useful and it contributes to your success with being a Data Protection Officer and your ongoing GDPR compliance. Please do take

Be an effective DPO

the time to share your feedback and suggestions on Amazon or connect with me on social media or on my website www.punitbhatia.com or mail me at engage@punitbhatia.com. Your inputs and feedback are highly appreciated.

Thank you so much for your time.

With best compliments…Punit Bhatia.

Annex

1. Job Description of Data Protection Officer

Below, you shall find a sample job description for DPO role:

DPO role description
As a DPO, your primary job is to assist the senior management by overseeing the strategy and implementation of GDPR and data privacy related practices. Your name and contact details will be communicated to the supervisory authority. You are expected to actively participate in the structuring and implementation of the strategic programs by providing advice on privacy and related matters.   As DPO, you shall lead an overall approach to privacy related policy and procedure development, training, communications and vendor management. As DPO, you will also be

Be an effective DPO

responsible for: risk assessments, data privacy impact assessment, and managing personal data breaches. You will also be defining and implementing compliance monitoring through relevant controls.

As DPO, you shall collaborate with stakeholders in business, IT, HR, procurement, Legal, Compliance, Risk and external parties.

Skills

- Strong communicator with excellent written and verbal skills
- Apt influencer with ability to advice senior and executive management
- Independent and intrapreneurial with ability to manage tasks and coordinate across variety of stakeholders
- Diplomatic for interaction with Supervisory Authorities
- Affinity for law and ability to connect and lead conversations on legal matters
- Self-motivated and collaborator who can find his way in the organization

Be an effective DPO

Qualifications
<ul><li>University Degree or equivalent, experience with CIPM/ CIPP-E certifications</li><li>Minimum of 5 years' experience in data governance and data management process on a senior level</li><li>Deep understanding of data and technology</li><li>Expert knowledge of national and European data protection laws</li><li>Knowledge of data security laws</li><li>Knowledge of market best practices, including in-depth understanding of GDPR.</li><li>Experience in managing third parties</li><li>Good understanding of operational processes, risk assessment, project management, information technologies and data security</li></ul>

Be an effective DPO

Data Protection Maturity Assessment

To review the GDPR situation that you have and find challenges with the current plan.

#	Topic	Score
1	Data Protection Policy	
2	Privacy/Protection Board	
3	Data Protection SPOC network	
4	Processing of personal data on the basis of a legitimate purpose	
5	Personal data retention periods	
6	Personal data retention approach	
7	Personal data post retention actions	
8	Individual rights for customers	
9	Individual rights for employees	
10	Individual rights for supplier personnel	
11	Individual rights request register	
12	Explicit and clear consent	
13	Processing of children's data	

Be an effective DPO

#	Topic	Score
14	Privacy Statement for customers	
15	Privacy Statement for employees	
16	Privacy Statement for supplier personnel	
17	Personal Data Breach notification	
18	Personal data Breach register	
19	Privacy by Design guidance	
20	Data Protection Officer assigned	
21	Data Protection metrics measured	
22	Third Party Management contract terms	
23	Third party management audit approach/procedure	
24	Data protection Awareness/ Training	
25	Data Protection Audit	

Against each of above, give your company a score amongst one of the followings:

1. If you believe that practices and processes in your company are not defined.

2. If you believe that practices and processes are somewhat defined but the actual procedures are based on a common-sense approach.
3. If you believe that practices and processes in your company are defined and staff generally follows these processes and procedures.
4. If you believe that practices and processes are not only defined and followed but also reviewed for improvements on a regular basis.
5. If you believe that practices and processes in your company are so mature that these are best practices for other companies to learn from.

Once, you have scored each of the items in a table; you should aim to work on things that are below a score of 3. And, in longer term, you shall target all aspects to be at 4 or above. You may also calculate an average and work on overall target.

Be an effective DPO

2. DPO Stakeholder list

A ready list of stakeholders for you to keep a check that all of them are being engaged.

Stakeholder type	Involved (Yes/No)
Board Members	
Employees	
Customers	
Supervisory Authority	
Legal Counsel	
Head of compliance	
Head of marketing	
Head of procurement	
Chief Data Officer	
Chief Information Security Officer	
Chief Enterprise Architect	

Note: Based on your situation, feel free to add or remove to above list and make your own list to check that you are engaging and connecting with right stakeholders.

Be an effective DPO

3. Sample Data Protection metrics

To measure key aspects of data protection compliance in your company.

Key Indicator	Description
Number of personal data breaches	To measure the number of personal data breaches that were detected in the specified period.
Number of DSARs*	To measure the number of data subject access requests that were made in the specified period.
Number of complaints to DPA	To measure the number of complaints that were made to Data Protection Authority in the specified period.
Number of data breaches reported to DPA	To measure the number of data breaches that were

Be an effective DPO

Key Indicator	Description
	reported to Data Protection Authority in the specified period.
% new clients who provided consent	To measure the percentage of new clients who opted in for the consent in the specified period.
Number reactions of privacy statement	To measure the number of customer requests or queries that were made on the basis of privacy statement in the specified period.
Number of open risk items from last data protection audit	To measure the number of risks (from last audit) that have not been closed yet.
Number of open high-risk items from	To measure the number of high risks (from last audit) that

Be an effective DPO

Key Indicator	Description
last data protection audit	have not been closed yet.

4. DPO Assignment Checklist

To review whether your company needs a DPO to be assigned or not, assess the following questions.

#	Criteria / Question	Yes/No
1	Does your company process a significant amount of personal data?	
2	Does your company process personal data at each step of your service provisioning?	
3	Are special categories of personal data involved?	
4	Does your company employees consistently create new products and services that include personal data?	

Be an effective DPO

#	Criteria / Question	Yes/No
5	Does your company employees need regular advice on data protection matters?	
6	Does your company's clients expect your company to be protecting the personal data of their clients?	

Pro Tip: If you have answered yes to most of the above, it is an indication that assignment of DPO can be a good step for your company.

5. DPO Breach Notification Checklist

To review your data breach notification template for completion.

Item	Included
Number of personal records impacted	
Number of data subjects impacted	
Description of likely impact of the data breach	
Proactive description of measures that were in place to prevent such breaches	
Name and contact information of Data Protection Officer	

About the author

Punit Bhatia is a senior professional with more than 19 years of experience in executing change and leading transformation initiatives. Across three continents, Punit has led projects and programs of varying complexity in business and technology throughout multiple industries. He has experience on both sides of the table; i.e., he has served as a consultant who worked for IT consulting companies, and also as a key influencer and driver who has defined and delivered change for large enterprises. He has proven expertise in areas of data privacy, sourcing and vendor management, and digital transformation.

Be an effective DPO

Punit is a Certified Information Privacy Manager (CIPM), Certified Information Privacy Professional Europe (CIPP-E), and Certified Outsourcing Professional (COP).

For last three years, he has been driving the compliance with **General Data Protection Regulation** (GDPR) in different roles. Part of this effort entails attendance in multiple events and dialogue with many experts. He has acquired knowledge and expertise in the field of data privacy and protection. Consequently, he is now active as a GDPR expert and as a speaker or panelist at different events. He is an author of the book "Be Ready for GDPR" that is available on Amazon in print and e-book versions.

Be an effective DPO

Acknowledgments

All the readers of my earlier book "Be Ready for GDPR" as you inspire me to write again.

Namita Bhatia (my wife), for being patient with my ideas.

Yash Bhatia (my son), for bringing new ideas and energy when a book is being written.

And special thanks to all my family, parents, colleagues, and friends who stand by me, work with me, and challenge me to learn every day.

Be an effective DPO

Make your own notes here

Be an effective DPO

Be an effective DPO

Be an effective DPO

Be an effective DPO

You may also want to read

Available on Amazon websites in e-book and print versions.

Made in the USA
Middletown, DE
16 July 2018